Children's Illustrators

David Wiesner

Jill C. Wheeler

ABDO Publishing Company

visit us at
www.abdopub.com

Published by ABDO Publishing Company, 4940 Viking Drive, Edina, Minnesota 55435.
Copyright © 2005 by Abdo Consulting Group, Inc. International copyrights reserved in all
countries. No part of this book may be reproduced in any form without written permission from
the publisher. The Checkerboard Library™ is a trademark and logo of ABDO Publishing
Company.

Printed in the United States.

Cover Photo: Houghton Mifflin
Interior Photos: Corbis pp. 10, 12; David Wiesner pp. 5, 7, 8, 13, 17, 23; Getty Images p. 11;
    Houghton Mifflin pp. 9, 15, 19, 21

Series Coordinator: Jennifer R. Krueger
Editors: Kate A. Conley, Stephanie Hedlund, Kristin Van Cleaf
Art Direction: Neil Klinepier

Special thanks to David Wiesner for providing photos for this project.

Library of Congress Cataloging-in-Publication Data

Wheeler, Jill C., 1964-
    David Wiesner / Jill C. Wheeler.
        p. cm. -- (Children's illustrators)
    Includes index.
    ISBN 1-59197-722-3
        1. Wiesner, David--Juvenile literature. 2. Illustrators--United States--Biography--Juvenile
literature. I. Title.

NC975.5.W5W57 2004
741.6'42'092--dc22
    [B]

                                                                                2004047718

Contents

Twisting Reality

Imagine an ordinary object, such as an orange. Imagine that orange as a beautifully painted piece of art. Now, turn the orange into something totally unexpected. Maybe it is a boat. Maybe the boat is really a fish. Imagine all of that, and you get an idea of David Wiesner's art.

Wiesner is best known for *Tuesday,* his 1991 tale of flying frogs. *Tuesday* takes ordinary frogs and gives them amazing adventures. The book exhibits one of Wiesner's favorite activities. He loves taking everyday things and turning them into **fantastic** stories.

Wiesner makes the kind of books he would have liked when he was a child. He knows children have wonderful imaginations. He makes sure his books encourage that. Wiesner's detailed, funny illustrations keep young readers entertained for hours.

Wiesner is always interested in doing the unexpected.

5

Always an Artist

David Wiesner was born on February 5, 1956, in Bridgewater, New Jersey. His father, George, worked at a chemical plant. His mother, Julia, was a homemaker. David was the youngest of five children.

David grew up watching his brothers and sisters draw. They sometimes gave him their old art supplies. David was thrilled to get boxes of pastels, bottles of ink, and tubes of paint. He began to draw and paint at a young age.

When David was just six or seven years old, he saw a television show about art. The show, *You Are an Artist*, was hosted by Jon Gnagy. David was amazed that Gnagy could create a whole picture in 15 to 20 minutes.

David's parents encouraged this interest in art. His family began to buy him art supplies for birthday and Christmas gifts. He loved to be inventive with these supplies. One time, he loaded paint into a squirt gun and fired it at a blank piece of paper to make art.

David's elementary school classmates quickly learned of his talents. He became known as "the kid who could draw." At home, he spent hours copying his favorite pictures of dinosaurs. He also copied cartoon and comic book characters.

A painting David did when he was five years old

It was not long before David knew he wanted to be an artist. He even wrote an essay about it in third grade. He wrote about the different kinds of paintings he wanted to do one day. David's teacher liked the essay.

Not all of David's teachers approved of his artwork, however. One teacher sent a note home to David's parents. She said he wanted to draw more than he wanted to focus on his schoolwork. Fortunately, David's parents continued to support his interest in art.

David had other hobbies, as well. His neighborhood was near several places to play. He and his friends spent hours playing army games in the nearby **cemetery**.

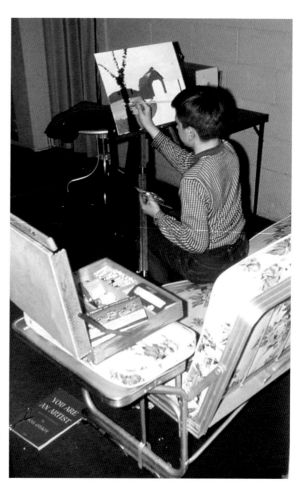

A copy of **You Are an Artist** *lies beside David as he paints at age 12.*

David and his friends also created homemade hot-air balloons from wire hangers and plastic bags. They launched the hot-air balloons through the neighborhood and pretended they were unidentified flying objects, or UFOs. In this way, David was already using his imagination to have fun with everyday objects.

David remembers his childhood adventures with hot-air balloons. They even appear in one of his books, June 29, 1999.

Getting Serious

David began thinking seriously about being an artist in high school. His art teacher was thrilled to have a student who loved art as much as David.

David had already studied many art books. He was in **awe** of works by **Renaissance** artists, such as Leonardo da Vinci and Michelangelo. He also enjoyed painters from the 1900s, such as Pablo Picasso.

David studied surrealist artists, such as Salvador Dali.

One day, a student from the Rhode Island School of Design (RISD) visited David's art class. It was the first time David learned there were special schools for artists. He decided that he would go to art school, too.

David graduated from high school in 1974. He was accepted to five different art schools. However, he chose to

Opposite Page: *Pablo Picasso's* **Mandolin and Guitar.** *With Picasso as an inspiration, it's easy to see how David's art is a little unusual.*

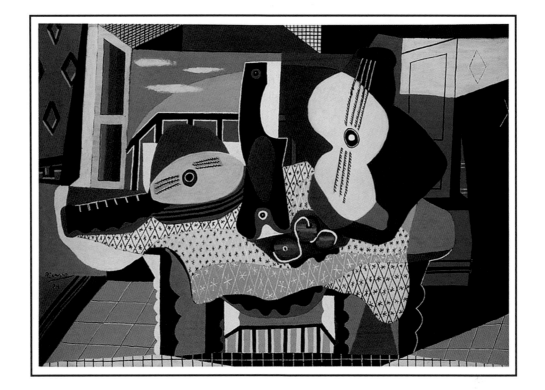

attend RISD. David spent his first years at RISD learning how to do things differently. He had to change some of his ideas about art. Yet, he realized this made his work even better.

One of his favorite projects involved painting about **metamorphosis**. David's painting begins with an image of an orange. The orange **segments** change into sailing ships, and the ground changes into water. Then the ships change into fish! David's classmates loved his painting. He knew he was on to something.

Illustrating for Children

Wiesner thought he would start his career creating art for adults. But, a RISD instructor encouraged him to talk to the art director of a children's magazine called *Cricket*. The meeting led to Wiesner creating the cover art for an issue of the magazine.

A courtyard at RISD. If it weren't for a RISD instructor, Wiesner may never have tried to illustrate for children.

Wiesner also got an **agent** for his art. Her name was Dilys Evans. Evans helped him get more jobs. In 1980, he was hired to do the illustrations for two children's books. One was called *Honest Andrew* by Gloria Skurzynski. The other was *Man from the Sky* by Avi.

In 1983, Wiesner married a young woman named Kim Kahng. In that same year, a fire destroyed everything they owned. For several years, Wiesner worked to meet **deadlines** as he struggled to rebuild his life.

Wiesner finally had time to do some work for himself in 1987. He and Kim worked together on retelling a fairy tale. *The Loathsome Dragon* was about a beautiful princess trapped in the body of a dragon. Book critics liked its **enchanting** artwork, which encouraged Wiesner.

David Wiesner in his studio

Free Fall

Wiesner began thinking about his next project. He showed some of his **fantasy** images to book editors. He asked if they could use pictures like his. They always said no. Wiesner realized he would have to write his own book to use his unusual pictures.

So, he created a book about the dream of a young boy. The pictures carry the boy from his bedroom to a giant chessboard, a castle, a city, and even a huge breakfast table. Wiesner called the wordless book *Free Fall*. It was published in 1988.

Wiesner was happy with the book. *Free Fall* was different from many other children's books on the market. That made some people uneasy. Yet, it made others enjoy the book even more.

The **Caldecott** committee chose *Free Fall* as a Caldecott Honor Book in 1989. That honor made Wiesner realize that he was on the right track. In the next year, he created another illustration for *Cricket* that would be an inspiration.

Wiesner remembers **Free Fall** *as his first project where he was doing what he really wanted to do. He didn't have to worry about matching his art with the text of another author.*

Flying Frogs

In March 1989, the editors of *Cricket* gave Wiesner a couple of options for a cover illustration. One option was to illustrate Saint Patrick's Day. The other option was to illustrate the issue's topic of frogs.

It was an easy choice for Wiesner. He chose to draw frogs because they are soft, lumpy, and funny looking. Now he had to decide what the frogs would be doing in the picture.

Wiesner began by taking out a sheet of clean, white paper. He sketched a frog on a lily pad in the center of the sheet. To Wiesner, the lily pad looked like a flying saucer. That gave him the idea for flying frogs. His *Cricket* illustration showed a group of frogs flying out of their swamp!

Wiesner then went to work on his next book. In *Hurricane*, a storm blows down a tree. Two boys think the tree is an amazing place to play. Their imaginations turn it into a jungle. *Hurricane* was published in 1990.

Wiesner's studio table holds a work in progress.

Elements of Art

Color

Color is one of the basic parts of art. Objects have color because they reflect or absorb light. The lightness or darkness of a color is called its value.

Wiesner uses many brilliant colors in his books. Watercolor is his favorite way of creating pictures. Watercolor uses color mixed with water instead of oil. This creates paint that is slightly transparent.

But Wiesner was still thinking about frogs. He began to imagine what would happen if frogs could really fly. One day he was on an airplane when he began sketching more frogs. One hour later, he had drawn the rough sketches for a book about frogs that can fly.

Wiesner worked with his editor to complete the final story. He studied photographs of frogs and made a clay model of one. Wiesner then made detailed drawings of every scene. He drew himself as a man who catches a glimpse of the flying frogs.

Next, Wiesner needed a name for his book. He decided it should simply be a day of the week. He chose Tuesday because it sounded like *ooze day*. That seemed just right for a story about frogs.

Tuesday was published in 1991. It was a hit from the very start. Critics noticed the detailed illustrations. Teachers liked the almost wordless story. Young readers loved to see the funny things the frogs were doing as they flew.

Opposite Page: *Wiesner has been fascinated with wordless storytelling since he was a teenager.* **Tuesday** *is an almost wordless picture book, with only the time of night used to narrate the story.*

TUESDAY

DAVID WIESNER

More Awards

Tuesday won the 1992 **Caldecott Medal**. Wiesner was not quite sure how to react at first. He realized that the list of Caldecott winners dates back to 1938. Wiesner soon felt very proud to be a part of that special list.

Wiesner's next books were *June 29, 1999* and *Sector 7*. *June 29, 1999* is about giant, falling vegetables. *Sector 7* is the story of a boy who visits a cloud factory. Once again, the books featured Wiesner's amazing watercolor illustrations. *Sector 7* was named a Caldecott Honor Book in 2000.

In 2001, Wiesner released a book called *The Three Pigs*. It is a retelling of the classic story. But this time, much more happens. The wolf blows the pigs right out of the story!

Like *Tuesday*, *The Three Pigs* won the Caldecott Medal. This time, Wiesner knew what an honor the award was. Wiesner and his wife now had two young children to celebrate with. They chanted, "Daddy won the Caldecott!"

Wiesner says he wants children to have fun when they read his books. His imagination is still at work today creating **fantasies** and wonder. He continues to entertain adults and children with his funny stories and amazing paintings.

Wiesner displayed his talent with watercolors in Sector 7, a story that is set in the clouds.

Glossary

agent - a person who represents authors or illustrators and helps them find work.

awe - a feeling of fascination and admiration.

Caldecott Medal - an award the American Library Association gives to the artist who illustrated the year's best picture book. Runners-up are called Caldecott Honor Books.

cemetery - a gathering of graves and their markers.

deadline - a set time before a project has to be finished.

enchant - to be very charming, as if to cast a spell.

fantasy - unusual or strange and beyond what is realistically possible.

metamorphosis - a process of slow and complete change.

Renaissance - a revival of art and learning that began in Italy during the fourteenth century, marked by a renewed interest in Greek and Latin literature and art.

segment - a piece of something.

Web Sites

To learn more about David Wiesner, visit ABDO Publishing Company on the World Wide Web at **www.abdopub.com**. Web sites about David Wiesner are featured on our Book Links page. These links are routinely monitored and updated to provide the most current information available.

Wiesner talks to a class about art in 1992.

Index